Simply Church

by Tony & Felicity Dale

Published in Manchaca, Texas, by Karis Publishing, Inc.

Karis Publishing, Inc.

PO Box 465

Manchaca, TX 78652-9824 USA

ISBN: 0-9718040-1-X

CONTENTS

WATCH OUT! A TIDAL WAVE IS COMING!

God is on the move! Jesus said, "Look around you! Vast fields are ripening all around us and are ready now for the harvest"(Jn. 4:35). We need to get the combine-harvesters ready!

Three years ago, we returned to England for the first time in several years. While we were there, God spoke to us very clearly and told us that we would have the privilege of being part of a powerful movement of His Holy Spirit for a second time. Back in the sixties and seventies, we had seen God move in extraordinary ways in England. Spontaneously, all over the country, churches had started in homes because people were so hungry to experience more of the Lord. Out of this, what became known as the "house church movement" was born. These churches now represent approximately one third of British evangelical Christianity. These churches, now known as the New Churches, often find themselves to be the largest church in town. Every little village and hamlet has one (or more). However, their influence extends far beyond their numbers. For some years we had been praying that we would again be allowed to be part of such a movement of God's Holy Spirit. Our hearts have desired that this would be a grassroots movement of "little" people—no superstars, no empire building, the Holy Spirit in control, Jesus alone lifted up, and all the glory going to Him!

In September of 2000, we traveled to India to do a series of conferences on church planting. We were teaching on material that we had used many times before, but God pushed us into a paradigm shift in our own thinking. We found ourselves genuinely believing, rather than just giving lip service, that churches could be planted rapidly. Perhaps it was because we were in an environment where we were hearing about the amazing things God is doing over there. One church planter told us that they now have a vision to plant a home church in every village in central India by the year 2007—a mere 17,000 villages! In American terms this would translate to a church in every apartment complex, neighborhood, school, retirement home, office block, hospital and factory! And we thought we were doing well if one of our home churches "multiplied" once in a year!

Since that trip, a number of things have happened. Stories from the people who attended the conferences have both humbled and blessed us. Within a couple of weeks of arriving home, we were getting reports of multiple churches starting. One lady, with a team of young people, had started four or five churches in the surrounding villages in just two weeks. Another young man had started two churches among his gypsy people in less than a month from the seminar.

Having heard these and other reports, we decided we had absolutely no excuse! So we took the plunge and have gone out over the past year and started many churches. They are very fledgling efforts at best, but at least they are there!

Let us share a couple of examples. One of the most exciting churches we have helped start is in a local, low-income housing project that our church had been praying for over a period of several months. ("Lord, deliver us from nice, white, middle-class churches!") We had decided to follow the principles we had been teaching in India, using

6

Luke 10 as the pattern. We were specifically praying that we would find the "man of peace." One day, while we were prayer walking in the apartment complex, we were caught in a sudden downpour. We found shelter under a porch with two ladies who lived within the housing project. We shared with them what we were doing. As a result, they invited us to go and pray with them about some of the problems the area was experiencing. Within weeks, both had given their hearts to the Lord! And Lily, the oldest of the two sisters, started to involve their families in a weekly time together with us. Isn't the simplest definition of church—"where two or three gather together" in Christ's name(Matt. 18:20)? Within months there were thirty to forty people meeting within Lily's apartment each week, and now another group has started from that first group.

Churches can multiply very rapidly. Recently, two couples have surprised us! One announced that they are about to start church for junior high kids in their area. Another pair, who have only been a part of the local home churches for around one month, told us that they are looking to leave the home church they have been a part of to start one in their own home. Wow! When the Lord puts church on people's hearts, it all comes together faster than we would ever imagine.

On a daily basis we are getting phone calls and e-mails from people all over the country saying that they are doing something similar! Here in Austin, groups that we had never heard of are emerging from the woodwork. All over this nation, people are saying the same things. The interest expressed by more traditional churches as well has been incredible. God is challenging His people to look at what the home church represents. It feels very similar to the early sixties as the Lord began moving in power in England. This needs everybody, both those in traditional settings and others who are already moving into new paradigms of church planting.

We love swimming in the ocean. When you are body surfing, you stand there waiting for "your" wave. You have to be in the right place, it has to be the right size and breaking at the right moment, and then you launch yourself out in front of it and kick for all you're worth, until the momentum of the wave carries you in to the shore. Our wave is out there. We're in the right place for it and it is just breaking, and this current move of the Spirit is gaining momentum. So let us share how this unfolding drama began for us as university students in the late sixties and early seventies.

We were medical students at Barts Hospital in London, England, and privileged to be part of an exciting move of the Holy Spirit. We had no idea then that we would look back on that time as a period of genuine revival. However, we now realize that what to us seemed very small, has ended up touching literally thousands of lives, both inside and outside the medical profession. This book, in part, tries to understand the roots of this period of revival. It seeks to explain why it has produced such long-term, meaningful change in people's lives.

As we look back, we realize there are many principles that we learned in those early days of working together that are still applicable to church life today. We were a bunch of young students. We had little idea of what we were doing or where this was going. However, we knew that the Holy Spirit was doing something wonderful and exciting, and we were prepared to follow where He was leading.

We now sense within ourselves a similar excitement over things we see emerging in the United States, as well as around the world. Recent contact with friends from Britain, and an increasing opportunity to see the good things that God is doing in many other parts of the world, gives us great hope for the future of the church.

It has been said that the one thing we can learn from history is that we never learn anything from history. The tragedy is that often this cycle has been replayed within Christian circles. In studying revival, it is not unusual to find that a group formed from a previous move of the Holy Spirit becomes an impediment to any subsequent moves of the Spirit. In the United States, there is currently a lot of interest in church planting. Our prayer is that as new models are explored, and as the Holy Spirit is allowed to have His way in multiplying many churches across the nation, those churches started in the last great church-planting wave will not be a barrier to the new churches now emerging.[1]

British society is now viewed as being a post-Christian culture. This shows how renewal within the churches over the last twenty years has only, so far, had a profound significance among God's people. Many have found the Lord and lives are being touched, but society itself has not yet been forced to sit up and take notice. What will it take to really change society? Much prayer has gone up for revival, but here in the West we have not yet seen what we are praying for.

Now you might say, "Isn't there a contradiction

to your comment that the late sixties and seventies were revival, and yet, ever since, everybody has been praying for revival?" I see no contradiction here. It is rather like the theological concept that the kingdom of God is here presently, and it has not yet come. God sovereignly did something by His Holy Spirit in the sixties and seventies that still bears fruit today. The large number of churches that have been established, along with the thousands of lives that have been changed, show all the hallmarks of the true revival of God. But this is still only a foretaste of what evangelical Christians in Britain have been praying faithfully for. The churches may have been touched and shaped by the charismatic and New Church movements, but society has not yet been changed in a meaningful way. That is a phase of revival that is still longed for.

In the United States the spiritual climate is very different. Culturally, it is still acceptable to be a Christian. In practice, however, there appears to be little difference between Christians and non-Christians, as is shown so clearly in Barna's book, *The Second Coming of the Church*. It is a sad commentary on church life when it can be shown that there is little, if any, difference between the world and the church in areas such as the number of people who watch pornography regularly, or the percentage of marriages that end in divorce.

How can the Christian climate now be transformed as it was in Britain during the sixties and seventies? We need a new wave of churches planted that challenge not only their own members, but also members of all evangelical churches to stand up and be counted for the kingdom of God. Recognizing that our current church institutions are not really touching society, could this transformation pave the way for society itself to be profoundly impacted by the kingdom of God?

In this context, what could two British medical doctors possibly offer that would help anyone understand church planting in the United States? Our experience is very limited, but we have been privileged over the years to see a number of churches start, and to see those churches exert an influence that is greatly disproportionate to their size. We have now lived in the United States for nearly fourteen years. Early in our stay we were part of four different churches of a more traditional nature. Those years of imbibing American culture and American church life have been very formative in what you will see written here. It was at the last of these four churches, Northwest Fellowship in Austin, Texas, that the pastors, Trey and Mary Anne Kent, strongly encouraged us to start something in the part of Austin where we lived. We were privileged to work with them and watch the very effective way that they were establishing new believers. When that church moved to the very opposite end of town to where we lived, it did seem that the timing was right to start something ourselves.

For two years we had been leading a Bible study group for business people to help them understand the importance of Biblical principles in dealing with finance. This had grown to the place where all of our non-Christian business colleagues who were coming regularly to this study had found the Lord. We then added a children's Sunday morning Bible breakfast club that we began for the sake of our own children. This group was made up of our own kids and their friends in the neighborhood. Most of those kids also became Christians. Various neighborhood friends who were parents of these kids also found the Lord. We then brought both of these groups together and started calling this "church." When that outgrew our house, we multiplied out into other homes. Now, there are around twenty of these house churches across south Austin.

We recognize that what we are currently doing in south Austin, in the heart of the Texas hill country, is just one expression among many that the Holy Spirit is using to birth churches across the nation. It appears to us that the Holy Spirit is stirring many in this country to see the need for new churches that follow new patterns. Ordinary people are recognizing that they have been called by the Lord to "go into all the world and preach the Good News to everyone, everywhere"(Mark 16:15).[2] The Bible has never known any distinction between clergy and laity. Since the giving of the law at Mount Sinai (Ex. 19:6) it has been clear that God desired a kingdom of priests. There was never a Biblical reason for separating lay from professional, full-time from part-time folk. All of us are called to "seek first the kingdom of God."

There are thousands of Christians who have given up on church, but who are still totally committed to following Jesus. Our desire in the publishing of this book is to help enable and empower them to go out and start churches. In these churches the focus will not be on buildings and programs and professionals, but rather on enabling "every member ministry." Instead of precious

14

resources being almost entirely used internally to maintain staff and building, those same resources can be used to fund missions and mercy ministries to a world that is waiting to see if the church can be relevant.

As you read on, imagine what would be possible if all of God's people got involved!

Tony and Felicity Dale
July 2002

CHAPTER ONE

PARADIGM SHIFTS

It was 1517 when Martin Luther posted his ninety-five theses and, in the process, changed the way Christians think about salvation by faith. At various times in history, seismic changes have come about over short periods of time. These changes are not gradual or planned out. Instead, they represent the convergence of ideas and technology in such a way that a dramatic shifting of opinion, a genuine new way of looking at things, emerges.

The current explosion of the Internet would represent such a paradigm shift. Within the space of a few short years, a concept within communications, along with the technology to undergird that concept, has emerged that is literally changing the way that people work, communicate and do business. When the Old Testament prophet Daniel said that in the last days knowledge would increase, he couldn't have had an inkling of how dramatically this increase would occur.[3] Millennia ago, it took several hundred years for the body of human knowledge to double. Now it doubles every seven years, maybe faster. The industrial revolution changed the face of England over the course of a generation. Recent advances in technology are allowing comparable changes to be made within months.[4]

Similarly, the life and practice of the church worldwide appears to be undergoing major changes. The 20th century alone has seen as much growth and change in the church worldwide as in all of the centuries from the end of the apostolic era through the end of the 19th century. Where does this place the church in America as we begin this new millennium?

Arthur Wallis, the elder statesman of the New Churches in Britain, gave a masterful explanation of church development over the centuries in his introduction to the book, *Another Wave Rolls In.* His analogy of the onward flow of the Holy Spirit's work through the church being like the incoming tide is powerful. What energy! What beauty and awesome power is displayed as the waves crash against the rocks. Nothing can stand in their way. Each wave represents a new truth unveiled that the church grasps. With the Reformation, that truth

17

was salvation by faith. With the Baptists, it was the importance of baptism by full immersion that came to the forefront. With the Pentecostals, the baptism in the Holy Spirit was once again brought to the attention of the whole body of Christ. God is progressively revealing truth (bringing new light from the timeless scriptures), so that He will have His way in His church, and one day His Bride will be without spot or blemish (Eph. 5:26).

It again appears that we are on the threshold of a time of seismic change within the American church. The 20th Century was the American century. However, as we look at the influence of the churches, it would appear that the impetus has moved from the first to the third world. Tremendous church growth in Asia and Latin America, with even more remarkable growth in parts of Africa, leads one to look outside the borders of the United States for the cutting edge of the Holy Spirit's work in this generation.[5, 6] Can the American churches again have the influence for the kingdom of God that would approximate to their size and financial clout?

George Barna, the well-known Christian pollster and writer, says in his book *The Second Coming of the Church* that there is a very strong case for the American church being currently on the edge of irrelevancy. His statistical data seems to suggest that the vast majority of American Christians have already moved to a place in their daily lives where being a Christian has little, if any, practical import. How different from being able to say, "These people have turned the world upside down!"[7]

American churches need to re-invent themselves if they are to be relevant to the baby boomers and the X and Y generations. Certainly, the changes cannot come at a snail's pace in this day of dot-coms and e-commerce. David Watson, a Christian leader of the last generation, cleverly parodied the famous hymn "Onward Christian Soldiers" to say, "Like a mighty tortoise, moves the church of God. Brothers we are treading, where we've always trod. We are all divided, many bodies we. Long in truth and doctrine, short in charity!"

The amazing thing about change, when it happens in God's time, is that in retrospect you can see it was all in His Word in the first place. King Solomon had it right when he said, "Nothing under the sun is truly new."[8] As we examine the extensive changes that are needed in the way we view church, it soon becomes obvious that we are just going back to the future. It's all there in the book of Acts. A management guru in the fascinating booklet *You?*

states that quantum leaps (major changes) often come just from looking in the right direction. The fly that keeps hitting its head on the window to try to get out of the room could save itself a lot of anguish if it turned around and saw that the door was open. So, if we in the churches just looked with fresh eyes (and open minds) at what is so obvious in scripture, we would find ourselves with the clarity that we need to see church re-invented in God's image rather than our own!

Nothing short of another reformation will be enough to release and to empower today's Christians to make an impact on this generation in the Western world. The time is past for gradual change. What else will prevent us from becoming totally irrelevant to the world around us? It is with these thoughts in mind that these two British doctors, presently in business rather than medicine as their means of tent-making, are trying, through the essays in this book, to offer a way forward.

We hope this is not presumptuous. For thirty-three years now, we have been involved through medical work, missions, and more recently, business, in the call to plant churches. Experience on both sides of the Atlantic has led us to believe that the revitalization of evangelical Christianity that has been experienced in the UK over the past thirty years can be, and should be, paralleled by an even more radical transformation of the church within the USA. God is no respecter of persons, and despite our obvious prejudices, He is not an Englishman!

So, let's look at some of the changes that are needed to remain faithful to what God is doing in His church worldwide, and to His word as revealed in the Bible.

CHAPTER TWO

LET'S KILL SOME SACRED COWS!

Never go to the movies on Sunday. If you don't wash your hands and say grace before a meal, God will give you a stomachache to punish you. Girls' dresses should be four inches below the knee, and boys' hair should be kept above the collar.

Sound familiar? Why are rules such as these associated with Jesus-centered Christianity? Christ didn't seem to mind His disciples plucking the ears of grain on the Sabbath. He didn't bother to ceremonially wash His hands before meals. All the pictures show Him with long hair, and well, I could go on and on. Jesus was not much of one for religious niceties.

How have we gone so far off course? How could those who would die for the infallibility of scripture be so lacking in the love of Jesus that they would happily (sometimes even angrily and publicly) separate from their brothers and sisters in Christ over such "key issues" as whether Jesus is coming back before or after the millennium, or whether or not spiritual gifts ceased with the apostles? Why can a dress code in a Christian school not allow a dress more than one inch above the knees, but the cheerleaders can come to class in skirts that *Playboy* would be proud of? Somewhere we are missing the boat. We evangelicals have become the descendants of the Pharisees of old, somehow equating our Christianity with externals while ignoring the internals. As Jesus said, "You strain your water so you won't accidentally swallow a gnat; then you swallow a camel!"[9] Since when was Christianity judged by "do this and don't do that," rather than by loving God with our whole heart, and loving our neighbor as we love ourselves?[10]

It all comes back to the paradigm through which we examine our faith. If my sunglasses are coated in green, then I will see everything green. If my Christianity is coated in externals and religious norms, then that is the perspective from which I will judge other Christians. For man looks on the outward appearance, but God looks at the heart.[11]

Maybe this is why we have become so good at the externals. Our meetings are more like performances. Who did we go there to meet anyway? Our worship often is more like a concert. Our preaching is like the debates of old. We go to church rather like we might go to a ball game. It makes a pleasant interlude in our overly busy schedules, and it provides some light relief in our otherwise stressful lives. But does it make a difference? Not if the statistics are telling the truth! I (Tony) believe that it was Samuel Chadwick, the great Methodist leader, who said, "The church that is man-managed rather than Spirit-led works no miracles."

When George Barna can write in *The Second Coming of the Church* that in studying the major social indices there is no statistical difference between evangelicals and the nation at large, we need to worry about whether or not the church is on the right track. While Christians are being imprisoned and dying *for* their faith in China and the Sudan and many other parts of the world, the church in the West seems to be dying *because* of our (weak) faith. What is wrong?

It comes back to what we are focusing on. Christianity is a way of life. Christianity is living as Jesus would live if He were in your shoes, which in fact He is! Anything other than this is just a religious system. Churchianity! We find ourselves doing what keeps the church happy rather than what keeps Jesus happy.

Paul warned about this when he told us to beware of anything that holds to the form of godliness while it denies the power.[12] A Christianity that apparently has the power to save but does not have the power to change lives is arguably not Christian at all.

Similar questions apply to church. Can something be the body of Christ,[13] the pillar and the ground of truth,[14] that which the angels longed to look into,[15] and yet be so man-managed and self-centered that Jesus is barely even allowed a look inside! As Tozer so aptly put it, "The church is like a constitutional monarchy, where Jesus is allowed the title, but has no authority to make any decisions."[16]

If the kingdom at its simplest level is any place where Jesus is the King, then how much of the kingdom does my life show? What does it mean for me, as for every Christian, to seek first the kingdom of God and His righteousness?[17] Is there something that makes being a pastor inherently more spiritual than being an actress or an attorney? Can I naturally assume that it is more spiritual to plan to be a missionary than a politician? How about being a youth pastor instead of a coach? I wonder which one has more influence in young people's lives?

In a powerful scene in the movie *Chariots of*

Fire Eric Liddell is challenged by his godly sister to forget the Olympics so that he can get on with the calling on his life to be a missionary to China. Eric's response is, "But God made me fast." So fast, in fact, that he first set a new world record in training for the 100 yards. He then set a world record in a race he hadn't even trained for when he had to run in the 440 rather than the 100 yards so that his race would not be on a Sunday. The whole world watched his stand for Christ in his unwillingness to run on a day that he felt would violate his conscience.

Our paradigm needs to shift to where we see all of life as service to God. When God called me to medical training, that did not make me any less (or any more) spiritual than His calling to my friend, Nick Cuthbert, to leave medical school to be an evangelist. Both have equal responsibility and equal opportunity in God's eyes.

By the same token, I am no more spiritual being in church than when I am seeing patients. In my experience, I may even be less spiritual, if I am playing along with the hypocrisy and judgmentalism that seems to be the norm in many church circles. At times, we have destroyed one another in the name of Jesus in deacons' meetings in a way that would have embarrassed our non-Christian friends if it had happened in a company board meeting. I think we Christians could have had a thing or two to teach the businessmen in the movie *Wall Street*!

How can we accept as normal the fact that the average Christian has never led anyone to Christ at work, at school, or in their neighborhood? What has so emasculated our church members that the title of Dawson Trotman's booklet, *Born to Reproduce,* sounds more like a campaign ad for large families than a description of the normal Christian bringing many others to Christ?[18] What have we done in our churches that leaves many Christians quite unable to even pray out loud, let alone obey Jesus' question, "Couldn't you stay awake and watch with me even one hour?"[19]

It is interesting that Jesus wrote no book, and left us no theological treatise. Instead, He gave us an example. He became the Word. We refer to the Bible as the Word of God, but the Bible itself points us to Jesus. Jesus states in John 5:39, "You search the Scriptures because you believe they give you eternal life. But the Scriptures point to me!" We produce courses for seminary students on systematic theology to prepare them for full-time Christian service. Jesus apprenticed twelve disciples by living with them for three and a half years to equip them for life. No wonder Paul comments, "The old way ends in death; in the new way, the Holy Spirit gives life." [20]

Christendom appears to have been beset from approximately the time of Constantine onwards with a fixation on the professional clergy class as opposed to the laity. Through the Dark Ages this divide was so marked that services were even forbidden in the vernacular,[21] as was translation of the scriptures, so that the laity could be deliberately kept in bondage to the professional clergy. The priest in this model becomes the mediator between laity and God. The Protestant model changed very little. Now the professional was allowed to marry, and the Bible was translated into the common language, but still the laity was kept from any place of authority, with true power residing in those who had been trained for professional (so called "full-time") ministry. What a far cry from tax collectors and fishermen who were the first apostles and church leaders!

The most explosive period of church growth was when laymen led the church. In truth, the New Testament knows of no laymen. A possible exception to this is the error of the Nicolaitans, mentioned in Revelation 2, which may be a reference to an early separation between professional church leaders and an increasingly disenfranchised laity.[22] This same thing is found throughout church history. The last century is replete with examples, from the growth of Pentecostalism worldwide, to the phenomenal expansion of the church under persecution in China over the past fifty years. When churches are freed from the shackles of needing a professional class to lead them, all of a sudden Mr. or Mrs. Average Christian finds that they are able to do and be all that God has been calling them to be!

Sitting in the average church, which is what my wife and I did for most of our first ten years in this country, opened our eyes to the incredible waste of talent that is represented by the people who fill the pews. Leaders of major corporations, people who run business-training seminars, and those who start up schools and factories are apparently not qualified to lead a Sunday school class. Even those who have been leading in other churches, and have spent time in Bible school, are left to waste in the congregation rather than be released into fresh ministry. No wonder the author of Hebrews could say to them, "You are like babies who drink only milk and cannot eat solid food."[23] We have helped our congregations stay infantile by treating them as infants. Mr. or Mrs. Average Christian can no more, in their current state, rightly divide the word of truth, than the average three-year-old can rightly divide up the Sunday chicken. After the first two years, the average Christian never brings a newcomer to church, and rarely, if ever, leads another person to the Lord. We condemn ourselves to perpetual childhood by a system that leaves all the power and responsibility for Christian growth in the hands of professionals, while the amateurs turn up for the show on Sundays, living the rest of the week as they please.

It is no surprise that the committed amateurs, finding so little outlet in the churches, turn their God-given talents and vision to such para-church structures as Bible Study Fellowship and Full Gospel Businessmen's Fellowship International. From what I (Tony) remember, our university meetings in groups like Campus Crusade and Inter Varsity often felt more like real church than what went on in the special buildings on a Sunday morning and Wednesday night.

So why, when we started admitting that these student meetings really were church, did it cause such a stir? Inadvertently, we were challenging the

sacred cow that church must take place in a consecrated building, led by consecrated people. Thinking of special buildings, didn't the church thrive in
its first couple of centuries without putting all of
that money into structures that would only be used
for a few hours per week? Come to think of it, the
churches under communist persecution seem to be
proving the same point!

The church clearly did very well without buildings and without many full-time leaders for the
first few centuries. Qualifications for leadership
included the ability to support one's self as and
when needed. The only promise was persecution,
not professional perks and public praise. Training
was in the school of hard knocks, not the seminary
of intellectual questioning. The simplicity of Christ
was valued, not scorned. The power of the Holy
Spirit was expected, not explained away.

There is a story, apocryphal I presume, told of
Thomas Aquinas being shown around the treasures
of the Vatican by the Pope. "Well, we certainly
can't say 'silver and gold have I none,'" comments
the Pope. "And neither can we say, 'In the name
of Jesus Christ of Nazareth rise up and walk!'"
exclaims Thomas. The contrast between the church
in the West and the churches in Third World coun-

tries would tell much the same story today.

It is time for Mr. and Mrs. Average Christian to start living as teachers like Watchman Nee envisioned in *The Normal Christian Life*.[24] When I first read that book it opened my eyes to how abnormal my own Christian experience had been until that point. Why do we accept as normal, and even try to defend, a practice of Christianity that has produced so few Christians who genuinely seek first the kingdom of God and His righteousness? It's almost as if we have turned that teaching of Jesus around so that we seek first all these things being added to us, and then we will have time to seek the kingdom.

So, what is the kingdom and where does the church fit in?

CHAPTER THREE

CHURCH AND KINGDOM

To re-invent the church, we first have to understand New Testament concepts of the kingdom of God. Again and again Jesus would tell the crowd, "For the kingdom of Heaven is like..." The Sermon on the Mount embodies the principles that Jesus wanted to see demonstrated in the lives of His followers. His public ministry begins with teaching on the kingdom, and ends in Acts 1 with Him again taking the time between the resurrection and ascension to talk "to them about the kingdom of God."[25]

We need to understand that "the earth is the Lord's, and everything in it. The world and all its people belong to Him"(Psalm 24:1). It's all God's! And He wants to redeem it all. Even creation, we are told in Romans 8, waits for its redemption along with the children of God. All of life needs to be redeemed. When I (Tony) worked in medicine, I had a responsibility to help redeem the "kingdom of medicine." If you are in law or business, social work or coaching, teaching or being a student, you still have a responsibility and opportunity to help redeem your world for the kingdom of God. Does this mean that we force the rules of the kingdom on others? Of course not! Jesus said, "My kingdom is not of this world."

We live "Thy kingdom come, Thy will be done on earth as it is in heaven." We demonstrate this by our godly lives, not by our professional power plays and arrogant demands. Rolland and Heidi Baker in Maputo opened up their lives and their home to a thousand war-torn orphans of Mozambique. Out of this sacrifice a massive church planting movement with around three thousand churches has emerged. This does as much to extend the kingdom of God in that country as years of classic missions work.

Doctors Trevor and Marion Griffith live in Plymouth, England. They set up community programs whereby patients with non-medical needs can get help from local Christian volunteers. For example, the home-bound elderly can get someone to help with their shopping. Again, the kingdom of God is being extended, and the local church—the body of Christ—is seen in action every bit as much as in a Sunday morning service. The program now has been extended far past the confines of just their medical practice, and is being copied in various other places in England.

Church is kingdom people in community. Community is not necessarily living together under one roof, but living with the type of relationship that fosters an active involvement in the needs of the world around us. The *ecclesia* ("called out") church of the New Testament is the peculiar (i.e. special) people of I Peter 2. America is so much the land of the free that we don't want anyone to restrict our freedom, not even for our brothers and sisters in Christ. We're family as long as you don't make any demands on me. Never expect me to put you and your needs in front of my right to my time, my possessions, my interests, and my needs!

To understand New Testament church life we need to see it in the context of the kingdom. These people were in the process of turning their world upside down. This was done neither through the ballot box, nor through the strength of an army. It was done through the overcoming power of love. They proved that the meek can inherit the earth and that you can overcome evil with good.

CHAPTER FOUR

THE KINGDOM NOW AND NOT YET[26]

A tension seems to me to underline the profound difference of expectation between differing understandings of the kingdom of God, and the degree to which we live in and experience this kingdom now. That God quite frequently does heal is nowadays really beyond speculation. Unless we feel that those who are reporting extraordinary accounts of the miraculous in various Third World countries (let alone folk like myself who have seen the Lord do a considerable amount of healing in this country) are lying, then we have little reason to doubt what God can do. If one wants documentation of God's healing power from well-attested sources, one can probably do little better than to read *Healing Miracles,* by Dr. Rex Gardner, FRCOG. However, the question is not what God *can* do, but what God *will* do.[27] Where do we draw the line between understanding what is ordinarily available to the Christian, and what is only available as an extraordinary manifestation of grace?

I believe the issue is clearly set out by our Lord in what we call "The Lord's Prayer": "Thy kingdom come, Thy will be done in earth as it is in heaven"(Matt. 6:10 KJV). We know that in heaven there is neither sickness nor dying, neither sorrow nor pain (see, for example, Rev. 21:4). A part of our task, as outposts of the kingdom of God on earth, is to be actively praying that the reality of that kingdom rule, which is now perfectly manifest in heaven, enters our earthly situations. It is obviously going to be a matter of both battle and perseverance for an open manifestation of this kingdom to come, whether it is in terms of "goodness and peace and joy in the Holy Spirit," or in the casting out of demons.[28, 29] Both are equally manifestations of the presence of the kingdom. Both are areas where we need to be involved aggressively in taking hold of Christ, but which will only be captured in this life as we pursue the Lord.

The Christian walk is not passive. Although Jesus is our righteousness, we are still commanded to "pursue righteousness." Although He is our peace, we are still told to "pursue peace with all men." Equally it is plain that "He is our life." This does not take away our necessity to reach out to

Him for this life. The degree to which we manifest the kingdom of God is going to depend on the extent to which we allow God's Word to take root in our heart. God's Word is equally valid to all people at all times. However, it only produces fruit in our individual lives when it is mixed with faith. The writer to the Hebrews remarks:

> God's promise of entering His place of rest still stands, so we ought to tremble with fear that some of you might fail to get there. For this Good News—that God has prepared a place of rest—has been announced to us just as it was to them. But it did them no good because they didn't believe what God told them. For only we who believe can enter His place of rest.[30]

Jesus taught us clearly that the kingdom of God suffers violence, and that the violent take it by force.[31] We play an integral part in this earthly manifestation of God's rule. This is typical of the whole realm of prayer warfare and what the Lord has taught us of prayer. Surely, it is not God who is changing as we pray, but we ourselves. Even as we pray, "Thy kingdom come, Thy will be done," we are effectively saying, "Lord, change me so that I can help extend the reality and answer of that prayer."

Perhaps I (Tony) can illustrate this with a situation from my own family's experience. A number of years ago when Felicity, my wife, and I were medical students, we had the opportunity of doing an elective period in the United States. While we were there, Felicity experienced a bacterial infection that was extremely painful. It was at a period in our Christian walk when we were seeking to learn much more from the Lord about healing. So, rather than just taking antibiotics (which would almost certainly have helped with the situation), we felt that we should pray. In seeking the Lord He made it very plain that this infection was at a spiritual level, a direct result of something being wrong in our lives. As we asked His forgiveness and turned away from this, the infection immediately cleared. A few weeks later the infection recurred. We went back to the Lord to ask Him why. He made it plain that this time it was not due to any sin but so that he could manifest His glory. The Lord told Felicity that at a specific time on a specific day the pain would go and she would be healed. To that very hour, what the Lord had promised happened.

At both times, we had to seek God and then pray His will into being. Is this not an expression of His command to us to pray "Thy kingdom come, Thy will be done, on earth as it is in heaven"?

There is no doubt that scripture makes it plain that there are limitations placed upon us. Although the sting of death has been taken away, the factor of death has not been removed. Our temporal bodies have not yet put on immortality. Creation itself, as is beautifully described by Paul in Romans 8, is still subject to both futility and decay. Our bodies are not excluded.

According to Romans 8:21, "All creation anticipates the day when it will join God's children in glorious freedom from death and decay." This verse seems to imply that the children of God are already enjoying a glorious liberty. The context is that of creation (i.e. the physical realm). One way, although certainly not the only way, of understanding this statement is that God's children are already enjoying a liberty in the physical realm, which will only subsequently be shared by the rest of creation. It's as if we, who are the firstfruits of redemption, are also experiencing the powers of the age to come in a way that is not yet available to the rest of creation.

This "being subject to decay" obviously affects Christian and non-Christian alike. Some Christians postulate that being a Christian is no more likely to protect one from a flu epidemic than if one were a non-Christian. Personally, I find this to be a puzzle. Simple obedience to the Word of God will protect us from venereal disease because our lifestyle will not promote it. A love of God's Word will lead us to honor our bodies, which are the temple of the Holy Spirit. This means that we are unlikely to smoke or drink excessively and so again, we find that we are protected from illnesses to which many non-Christians succumb. My own experience of much pastoral work within the church has led me to think that the prevalence of anxiety and depression within it is substantially different to that within the world at large. I do not mean to imply that it is not there. Any pastor knows that it is, and in abundance. However, the answers are there as people move more into the peace and joy of Christ, and so they find their anxiety and depression lifting.

There are some very interesting but anecdotal, rather than statistically valid, accounts that can be gleaned from Christian writings regarding the public health effects of local, powerful healing ministries. Approximately 250 years ago, in a district of Germany, a Godly pastor by the name of Bloomheart took over the responsibility of the local parish church. Over the thirty years that he was in that district, he exercised a powerful ministry of healing and casting out demons. It was said of that district that it enjoyed better health than any of the other districts in Germany.

Perhaps more verifiable in the modern scientific sense are accounts of the life and ministry of such men as John G. Lake.[32, 33] This remarkable Christian business entrepreneur was called of God first to South Africa, where he established the rapidly growing and influential Apostolic Faith Churches, then later returned in the late 1920's to the state of Washington. Here, based in Spokane, he exercised a powerful healing ministry over a period of five years. It is recorded that 100,000 medically verified healings took place under his ministry during that five-year period. A Washington state senior public health official commented that "the health of the whole region had been affected by John G. Lake's ministry." It is at best speculation to state how this happened. Had the powers of darkness somehow been rolled back from a particular geographical location for a period of time? We may not yet see everything in the Spirit clearly, but we can certainly see some of the effects. Jesus himself, describing the work of the Holy Spirit, said that we may not see (or understand) all that He does, but we would certainly see His effects even as we see the effects of the wind in the trees.[34]

2 Corinthians 4:12 says, "Death is at work in us, but life is at work in you." This very interesting passage seems to underline the pressures that all those in Christian leadership know are part and parcel of our following the Lord Jesus Christ. Somehow, the very pressures that we work under produce their own toll, whether that be at a mental, emotional, spiritual, or physical level. It is into this context that Paul says, "Though outwardly we are wasting away, yet inwardly we are being renewed day by day. For our light and momentary troubles are achieving for us an eternal glory that far outweighs them all. So we fix our eyes not on what is seen, but what is unseen. For what is seen is temporary, but what is unseen is eternal."[35] However, this is no willing surrender to increasing decay, so much as joyful and obedient sacrifice for the sake of others. Earlier in this very passage, after Paul emphasizes that what is eternal is clearly more important than what is temporal, he tells us, "We who are alive are always being given over to death for Jesus' sake, so

that His life may be revealed in our mortal body."[36] It is the actual life of God which is finding expression, not just through our spiritual existence, but also our physical life. This was the great revelation that the founder of the Christian and Missionary Alliance, Dr. A. B. Simpson, had when he himself was crippled through overwork and pulmonary disease. In his understanding that Christ was his life, he was able to take hold of healing. He worked from that day onwards with a renewed strength and vigor that had never been his, even in his earliest days in the ministry, when he was exceedingly fit. The subsequent tremendous growth of the Christian Alliance through the United States and across the world says volumes for this saintly man of God. Many other spiritual giants have emerged from this denomination that had its roots in A. B. Simpson's revelation of the glory and power of the risen Christ: F. F. Bosworth (who conducted massive healing crusades across the United States and Canada in the beginning of the 1900's) and A. W. Tozer (whom many consider one of the most spiritual "prophets" of recent years) are of a few of the most well-known.

So, why then do we go so often without this apparent "liberty" that is available to the believer (i.e. the liberty of health and healing)? There are a number of reasons:

1. The lies of Satan. Satan is a liar and the father of lies. If there is some way that he can work out his task of seeking to "steal and kill and destroy,"[37] then he will do just that. He will lie within our minds and within our bodies. Perhaps the greatest lie that he has perpetrated on the church is that Christ's salvation is really only effective for our spiritual needs. He has left us blind to the glorious truth that our God wants to make us complete in every way—spirit, soul, and body.[38]

2. The kingdom not yet fully realized. It is not enough though, just to say that Satan has kept God's people in bondage. I think we have to realize that we now experience in only an incomplete and imperfect way the promise of the kingdom. We are still praying as our Lord taught us to pray, "Thy will be done, on earth as it is in heaven." That kingdom is neither fully realized nor perhaps even fully anticipated by us in this present age. It is this lack of faith that leads us to the third area.

3. Low level of faith and expectation in the church. Lack of clear Biblical teaching over many generations has led to the extremely low expectation of health and healing that is now the norm in the body of Christ, the church. In addition, modern scientific medicine has effectively become a religion of its own, with most of the church willingly bowing down at the altar of what the doctor says. There is little wonder that we see such lack of health in the church. The doctor has replaced the priest as the foremost prognosticator of future events. His "divine" ability to give a prognosis has become a type of negative prophecy that usually inspires despair and fear in those who receive it.

4. *As believers we do not need to expect that the coming of illness will necessarily have a natural course and outcome.*[39] We live as believers, not only within the natural realm, but also in the whole realm that is pervaded by the Spirit of God. When confronted with the reality (or fact) of sickness, we do not give in to the medical prognosis any more than we expect to give in to our feelings when we feel anxious, low, or angry. Instead, it is right at this point of vulnerability that we reach out to God in faith and take hold of the promises of His Word. We can challenge the powers of darkness through aggressive prayer that God will restore us to full health.

CHAPTER FIVE

SO, WHAT IS CHURCH?

Church is "where two or three gather together because they are [Christ's]"(see Matthew 18:15-20 for Jesus' teaching on this). At the simplest level, what more do we need? Jesus is present. Where the King is in residence, the kingdom cannot be far behind. That is why a Bible study group at work is probably closer to real "church" than the place that we may go to on Sunday. Here we see the reality of each other's needs. Here we know when someone loses his or her job, or the struggle when a colleague's child is seriously ill. Here we rub shoulders, and overcome real-life issues and challenges in an environment that will show whether or not we really care. Here we can do more than read out your name along with a dozen others who have their birthdays this week.

It is interesting that the most rapid church growth worldwide is nearly always associated with churches that are finding a way to meet in small groups based around their members' homes. I remember how challenged and impressed Felicity and I were in visiting Dr. Paul (David) Yonggi Cho's church in Seoul, South Korea in the early eighties. At that time, about 350,000 people were one church, yet meeting in tens of thousands of homes on a weekly basis, where they could be individually discipled, encouraged, and prayed for.

Small groups can similarly start overnight, as was demonstrated by our recent experiences in Mozambique. We would travel for a few days of medical work in a remote village. If we could find any Christians in the area, we would meet with them. Together, we would hold evangelistic meetings in the evening under a tree. Literally hundreds of people were giving their lives to Jesus. We could then help organize them into a community of worshipers, growing in the things of God without any building or full-time workers to stay among them. By making sure that they are in contact with apostolic and prophetic people in their country, we could ensure that they establish foundations that will, in time, see them becoming mature churches, reaching out to others.

It is neither the building, nor the pastor, that makes a church legitimate. It is the presence of

Christ among his people. A handful of new Christians in Mozambique, meeting in one of their mud huts for fellowship, study, and prayer, while sharing their limited food, seems more like church than a thousand people in one of our "cathedrals" being entertained by a few professionals for ninety minutes on a Sunday morning.

In New Testament times, we see Paul and his teams often being only a short time in a location before persecution or the prompting of the Holy Spirit forces them to move on. Why, when they came back a few months or years later, could they find a growing, maturing church? Two points stand out. Firstly, they trusted the young converts to God. Theirs was not a theoretical dependence on the Holy Spirit, but a practical reality. If God did not lead these young converts on, then neither would anyone else. Secondly, they trusted the young converts to be self-governing and self-directed. The helping hand of traveling ministries was an adjunct to their growth, not the essential condition of that growth.[40]

When Christians live life in the light of the call to seek first the kingdom, then all parts of their lives come under the scrutiny of the Holy Spirit. Suddenly the issue is not, "Do you tithe?" but rather,

"What do you keep?" After all, "God bought you with a high price. So you must honor God with your body."[41] The practical application of this approach to church life is that huge resources can be released into the kingdom of God. When a church is not encumbered with endless building programs, and yet more staff, it is amazing what can be released to missions, or to care for the poor and needy. It is not unusual for churches of this type to be able to release seventy or even eighty percent of their income to reach out to those outside the church, rather than just to maintain those inside it.

One church leader we know who was in a well-known mega-church, told us of the situation that caused him to drop out of leadership. He was in the leadership meeting of the church, with its million-dollar budget, when he realized the church had nothing available that it could use to help a young couple that had lost their jobs just before Christmas. Something was wrong when they could put up fancy buildings, and run expensive Christmas programs, but could not care for their own.

Stories like this force us to ask, "What is church?" It is interesting to note that the New Testament describes only three types of churches, and of these, Jesus only mentions two.

First, there is the church universal, made up of all Christians all over the world in all times and places. Jesus says of this church, "All the powers of hell will not conquer it"(Matt. 16:18).

Secondly, there is the church in the home, the small gathering of believers that Jesus refers to in Matthew 18:15-20 as the place of church discipline, and which He defines as where "two or three gather together because they are Mine." The continued emphasis on the small gathering is seen from the beginning of Acts (see Acts 2:42-46), through the various churches in homes mentioned in the epistles, to the end of Paul's ministry which ends up with him ministering in his home to groups of believers (see Acts 28).

The third and final description of church comes repeatedly in the epistles when the writers refer to the church in a locality, such as Jerusalem or Ephesus. This local expression is made up of all Christians in that area, whether or not they meet together.

I live in south Austin. But the "church" that I am a part of is not by itself the church of south Austin. All people who love our Lord in south Austin are a part of that church. Commuting across town to fellowship with people for an hour or two (who happen to mainly agree doctrinally with what I believe) is only a caricature of real church life. Did Peter and Paul cease being a part of the church just because they had a strong disagreement (see Galatians 3)? If you have ever participated in a March For Jesus in your city, you have probably seen a closer expression of the church in your city than any denominational model including "non-denominational"! It is so encouraging reading about church leaders, among many others, gathering across the denominational divides and praying for their towns and cities. Many so-called "city reaching" experiments are being tried, with considerable success, to help Christians in a locality see that they are all a part of the same body of Christ.

So how should Christians function when they come together?

CHAPTER SIX

WHEN YOU COME TOGETHER

How can we know what our pattern should be when we come together?[42] This is a most interesting question when considered in the light of the remainder of 1 Corinthians 14:26. Paul here answers his own question, "One will sing, another will teach, another will tell some special revelation God has given, one will speak in an unknown language, while another will interpret what is said..." Why is it that so few of our meetings actually work like this? It appears that as the program has come in, the Holy Spirit has been forced out! I believe that it was George Fox, the founder of the Quakers, who refused to start preaching until "the Holy Spirit came upon him," even if that meant standing in the pulpit silent for long periods of time. How sad that Quaker meetings are now primarily known for their silence rather than for the passionate preaching that should follow the silence!

Most of us who have experienced small group

life (whether in a university Christian group, a home church or a cell group) look back to those times when "each one *was allowed to* have" something to contribute to the meeting with great fondness. For many, their experience of Christ in a Navigator Bible study group, or a meeting of Campus Crusade, or a small prayer meeting at the office has spoiled them for what then happens in real life at church. All of a sudden, instead of active participation, and the bonding that comes through mutual discovery, most Christians find themselves like puppets at a show. As Vance Havner, a great Baptist preacher of a previous generation said, they are "like wooden Indians at a baseball game."

We just came back from a series of conferences and seminars in India teaching these principles of home church life and meeting to many groups of Indian pastors. To demonstrate what we were talking about, we broke the conferences down into smaller groups of eight to ten people for times of Bible study and prayer. First we explained some simple patterns of interactive Bible study (see Appendix 1). Then, within their small groups, we gave them twenty-five to thirty minutes to study the book of Philemon, using one of the interactive methods that they had just learned. When they then came back together, we again and again saw them excitedly agreeing on the following:

• They had just learned more about Philemon in half an hour than they previously had learned in their whole Christian life. (Don't forget that these were groups of pastors!)

• What they had learned was practical and down to earth.

• They had barely had time to get started on the book, let alone cover it in any depth.

• Everyone had wanted to actively participate.

In our own experiment in pioneering home churches in Austin, Texas we determined from the start that people would not be allowed to sit as spectators in meetings, but that all would be actively drawn in. For our first two years, I (Tony) don't think any of the people in the church saw or heard a "sermon." Everything, including any teaching, was done in a highly interactive fashion. Each week, different people would come with a simple, five-minute teaching which was followed by active discussion applying it into our daily lives. Sometimes it would be next to impossible to figure out who was leading in a meeting. What matters is that Jesus is seen as the center of the gathering. Worship and praise, learning of Him, are core to all we do.

My cousin Frances was living with us at the time that a close friend of hers, from her high school days in Hong Kong, was going to be visiting us. It was very important to Frances that her friend would really enjoy coming to this Sunday morning meeting. We all knew that sometimes the Sunday meetings got rather rowdy. So we were all saying, "Well Lord, please this week don't let anything too unusual happen. We know that Frances' friend won't understand."

You see, he wasn't a churchgoer; he wasn't even a Christian. We knew he would easily be put off if there were things that he viewed as "weird" and "emotional."

The meeting began in the normal way with some singing and praise. Carl was playing the guitar with his usual vigor. Whether he had broken a string by this time, I have no idea. He seemed to break one almost every meeting. People were joining in, lots of different people were either starting choruses one after the other or leading out in prayer. There was a real sense of the presence of God. And then I saw my friend Richard stand up. My heart sank. I had seen this before. As he stood there with his hands raised up in the air praising God, suddenly he collapsed in a huge heap on the floor. There was no way not to notice it. And yet everybody just ignored him. They continued to worship, and praise, and sing, and give glory to God. As I looked over with an anxious look towards Frances' friend, I saw him obviously overwhelmed by the presence of God.

I asked him after the meeting how he had found the time. His reply was "I never knew the presence of God could be so real."

There are many things about worship and praise that we don't really understand. But clearly, worship is foundational in scripture. We have a whole book devoted to the songs of worship and praise of the ancient Israelites, namely the Psalms. We have many accounts throughout the New Testament of the disciples or other followers of the Lord being involved in worship and praise. We know how Michal despised the way that her husband, David, danced so uninhibitedly in worship and praise before the Lord. This was enough for God to bring barrenness to Michal. We know that a love of worship and praise characterized David as "a man after God's own heart."[43]

I think a starting place in understanding worship and praise would be a quick look at Romans 12:1. There is far more involved than singing some well-known choruses or people clapping their hands! Worship is the only appropriate response of the creature to the Creator. It's the natural response of the human heart touched by God. It's a response that doesn't show itself primarily through adoration and praise, but more specifically by a life really consecrated to God. This passage states, "I urge you, brethren, by the mercies of God, to present your bodies a living and holy sacrifice, acceptable to God, which is your spiritual service ofworship."[44] Worship is only reasonable when it first implies a giving of ourselves to God. Part of the reason that much charismatic worship appears so shallow is that it really cannot transcend the shallowness of many people's lives. To think that we can be jumping up and down in a meeting, and then steal from our employer by not giving of our best is a contradiction in terms. Jesus made this very plain when He taught us through the apostle John that if you cannot love your brother who you can see, how can you pretend to love God whom you can't.[45]

Worship is a lifestyle. It's an indication of a heart bowing down before the Creator. Worship, as it is expressed in meetings, is only an extension of worship as it is expressed in our daily lives. This was powerfully brought home to me once in my teenage years.

I had been working for the summer in a Christian camp in upstate New York. The work in the kitchens was fairly hard and had long hours, but was more than compensated for by the quality of the meetings in the mornings and evenings. It was a time when the Lord was teaching me much, and increasing my understanding of what it meant to follow the leading of the Holy Spirit.

On this particular day there was a switchover of kids who were coming to the camp. Because many of the other young adults who were working in the kitchens had friends that were arriving that day, everybody had left the kitchens. Since I was a British student, just over for the summer, I didn't know any of these new kids coming in, so I stayed in the kitchen to finish clearing up. I was working on the big pots and pans feeling a little bit sorry for myself. I was lonely and wishing that I had friends coming just as everybody else seemed to. As I was there thinking these thoughts, I realized that what

I had been learning in the meetings was encouraging me to praise and worship whatever the external circumstances. So, I began singing and praising the Lord.

Meanwhile, unnoticed by me, the bus driver that had brought up the new batch of kids from the city had come down to the kitchen. He made himself a sandwich and was eating. Suddenly, I heard a voice from the other end of the kitchen. "What are you so happy about?" I turned around and saw the bus driver, and I went over to chat. As we shared, I had a wonderful opportunity to share God's love with him and discuss all the good things that the Lord was teaching me at this camp. As I reflected on that later, I realized in my attempt to glorify the Lord through praise and worship that I had allowed the Lord to come into my situation to bless both me and the bus driver. The issue is not whether we have a preference for liturgy or modern choruses, for ancient hymns or for spontaneous prayers. Rather, what has the Holy Spirit, through His Word, the Bible, taught us?

King David talks about this in the Psalms. Most of us have experienced how coming before God in praise releases an awareness of the presence of God in a most beautiful way. Praise opens the door for the King to come in. It specifically tells us this in Psalm 24:

> Open up, ancient gates!
> Open up, ancient doors, and let the King of glory enter.
> Who is the King of glory?
> The Lord, strong and mighty, the Lord, invincible in battle.

The gateway into the presence of God is through praise. In the book of Revelation we read that the heavens are filled with the praises of God. The four and twenty elders, the living creatures, among other beautiful pictures that we may not fully understand, all show God's creation lovingly worshiping and praising Him throughout eternity. We are given the privilege of joining with this heavenly chorus in giving honor and glory to God.

But there is more to praise and worship than just being in the presence of God in a meeting. Praise is a choice. It's a way of life. It tells us in Philippians 4 that we should "rejoice always." This isn't just a pious platitude, but an invitation to live in the presence of God. In Nehemiah 8:10 it says, "The joy of the Lord is your strength." At many times, when I've wondered how to carry on, I have found that lifting up my heart in praise has renewed and invigorated me to continue whatever God had given me to do. Many times I've gone into a meeting tired and exhausted and feeling like I had nothing to contribute. Then, as I allowed myself to be caught up in the worship and praise, I would find my body and my soul soaring with new strength and vitality. It is always a privilege to enter again into the presence of God through our worship.

It seems that there are really only two languages spoken throughout the world. And, no, I don't mean English and everything else! These two languages are worship and praise as contrasted with grumbling and complaining. One of God's chief complaints against the Old Testament people was how frequently they found reason to grumble. It seems like Christians are little different now. The typical language when people get together, whether at home or in the office, or sadly even in Christian meetings, is one of grumbling and complaining, finding what's wrong.

I know in England, where I come from, it is a national pastime to talk about how bad the weather is. The whole idea of constantly speaking upbeat, positive words that are trying to build a person up would be foreign to many people. But the Word of God teaches us: "In everything you do, stay away from complaining and arguing, so that no one can speak a word of blame against you. You are to live clean, innocent lives as children of God in a dark world full of crooked and perverse people. Let your lives shine brightly before them."[46]

If this is the call of God in our lives, then we need to be an example. We have the opportunity to live every moment in praise, and the results are phenomenal. Again and again I've seen in myself, and read in books about others, how praise drives away the doubt and the fear, the discouragement and the depression. Merlin Carothers' book, *Prison to Praise*, has not only challenged me, along with millions of other Christians, but I have seen it lead to transformation in the lives of hundreds of my patients.

King David understood the foundational nature of praise to help us live in the presence of God. The Psalms are full of David's poetry of praise. "The heavens tell of the glory of God. The skies display His marvelous craftsmanship."[47] No wonder this man of God could be quoted as saying, "I know the Lord is always with me. I will not be shaken, for He is right beside me."[48]

It is this understanding of living in the Lord's

presence continually that needs to permeate all of our times of coming together as God's people. The term "having a meeting" may be a misnomer, but it does state what, sadly, is not always obvious: that we are coming together to meet with Jesus. The question of leadership is really just a question of how can we make sure that the Holy Spirit is given the room to make Jesus the leader of all of our lives, whether together or individually.

CHAPTER SEVEN

WHO'S THE BOSS AROUND HERE ANYWAY?

In our experience, we have found that whenever Felicity and I go away on mission trips, invariably the local churches have grown, and sometimes even multiplied into new groups in our absence. In the New Testament church models, it was not unusual for a church to send out its best, its leaders. Look at the church in Antioch sending out Paul and Barnabas.[49] As we follow the ministry of Paul we see that often he would stay in a city for only a few weeks or a few months. Yet at the end of this time, he could trust the Holy Spirit to lead through the people who were left behind. We would never consider sending out the senior pastor and leaving the church in the hands of the youth minister or elders! So, how do current ideas of church leadership actually fit with the Biblical models that were left for us from the New Testament?

In the late sixties and early seventies, the Holy Spirit was moving powerfully on both sides of the Atlantic. In the States, it was the days of the Jesus movement. The emphasis brought by the Holy Spirit into many American churches was of God's supernatural power. Many unusual healing ministries were released, new church movements were birthed, such as Calvary Chapel and Vineyard, along with much of the church being challenged by the faith movement. In the UK, the emphasis was different, with the charismatic movement leading into an understanding of the importance of being the body of Christ. Church structure and government came to the fore, as God raised up apostolic and prophetic ministries to call the church to repentance and faith. The emphasis tended to be on character rather than charisma. Both countries have a lot to learn from each other. The strengths on one side of the Atlantic tended to be the weaknesses on the other. How to learn from and build on each other's strengths is the challenge.

One of the most controversial issues surrounding the type of church life that we are discussing is that of leadership. Some people feel that the church does not need any kind of structured leadership— that if the church consists of small groups, they do not need to designate any specific leadership. However, the New Testament church did appoint leaders, some of whom exerted very strong leadership at times. At the other extreme is the CEO, business-style leadership, where one man has the vision and carries the authority to work that vision out. The development of the "mega-churches" with their large staffs and polished programs would typify this style of leadership, which has become the norm for "successful" churches in the States. However, this kind of leadership is also difficult to show in the New Testament. So, what was the nature of leadership in the early church?

A quick read of the New Testament leads one with no doubt as to who was in charge of the church. It was Jesus, working through the Holy Spirit! Colossians 1:18 states, "Christ is the head of the church, which is His body." The book of Acts makes it plain that this was worked out in practice. For example, Acts 13:2 says, "One day as these men [the prophets and teachers of the church in Antioch] were worshiping the Lord and fasting, the Holy Spirit said, 'Dedicate Barnabas and Saul for the special work I have for them.'" The anticipation was clearly that God would guide in the practical, day-to-day life of the church.

So, what we are really looking for in church leadership is a context that allows the Lord to lead. This is not a democracy, neither is it a CEO-type leadership. Rather, it is a style where Jesus Himself is welcomed to lead His church. How can that actually happen in this day and age? Isn't that just pie in the sky? Our experience is that this is not only possible, but eminently practical. We just need a new look at the nature of authority as lived and taught by Jesus.

In Matthew 20:25-28 Jesus states:

> You know that in this world, kings are tyrants, and officials lord it over the people beneath them. But among you it should be quite different. Whoever wants to be a leader among you must be your servant, and whoever wants to be first must become your slave. For even I, the Son of Man, came here not to be served but to serve others, and to give My life as a ransom for many.

Jesus was the supreme example of servant leadership. Paul gives us some insight into this leadership style when he says, "But we were as gentle among you as a mother feeding and caring for her own children. We loved you so much that we gave you not only God's Good News, but our own lives too"(1 Thess. 2:7-8). And Peter, giving advice to the elders in I Peter 5 states, "Care for the flock of God entrusted to you. Watch over it willingly, not grudgingly, not for what you will get out of it, but because you are eager to serve God. Don't lord it over the people assigned to your care, but lead them by your good example." It is clear throughout the New Testament that authority is of a servant nature, willing to submit to others, gentle and loving, and ready to lay down one's life for others.

On a variety of occasions we have seen what this means in practice. A number of years ago, Tony had a clear sense that the Lord was leading us to start a Christian school as a part of the work of the church. We worked at the time in the East End of London; an inner city area that most Christians left as their kids grew older because the schools were so bad, both academically and spiritually. The leadership team was with him in this desire, except for one person. For important decisions, our pattern was to wait until there was a clear unanimity. We trusted the Holy Spirit that He would give the green light when He brought us to the place of being of one heart and one mind. At the right time, in an amazing way, when the Lord was also going to make a superb property available to us for the school, this "common mind" came to all on the leadership team. Contrast this with the "senior pastor" concept that is normal in American churches. In one of the first churches that we were a part of in the States we were told in no uncertain terms that the vision was the pastor's and everyone else was to support the pastor's vision. We have found that this pattern exists in practice in most American churches. There is a CEO who definitely has the first and the final say. The interesting thing is that both the senior pastor and the congregations seem to like it that way. Our impression has been that the adulation that is received by many senior pastors is close to idolatry. Of course, we should respect our leaders. That is both natural and Biblical. But we had better be careful about putting them on pedestals, or they might fall off. Remember Humpty Dumpty!

Note the warning Jesus gives religious leaders of His day, "Don't ever let anyone call you 'Rabbi,' for you have only one Teacher, and all of you are on the same level as brothers and sisters. And don't address anyone here on earth as 'Father,' for only

God in heaven is your spiritual Father..."(Matt. 23:7b-9) Yet in the evangelical/charismatic world of today, the pastor loves to be called "pastor." The people who hang on his every utterance place him on a pedestal. This idolatry is not entirely the senior pastor's fault. The church culture of today teaches the people to have this kind of attitude towards its leaders. This is unfair. No wonder so many pastors end up acting as CEO's rather than as the servants they were called to be. As the paid professional, they are not only expected to hear God about the direction of the church, but also to hear from God on a weekly basis for the Sunday and Wednesday night sermons, to organize the programs, visit the sick, and run a perfect family life too! It is not surprising that many, trying to live up to this impossible image, end up shipwrecked morally or physically.

It reminds me of the respect that was shown to us when we worked as doctors. Put on that white coat (and make sure that everyone can see your stethoscope) and you automatically become the leader, the boss. That kind of respect is only skin deep. It is character that makes the person, not position. The trouble is that it is rather fun being given that respect, even when it may not be deserved. When

Tony began working within American churches, he inadvertently caused considerable problems for the pastors that he was working with by refusing to let the people call him "pastor" or "doctor." He didn't want, and wouldn't accept, the prestige that comes from the position. Church leaders need to gain respect by laying down their lives rather than by upholding their position.

Part of the problem here is that this pattern of church, with a senior pastor as the main leader, is not a scriptural model. In fact, the term "pastor" as such, is only used once in the New Testament, in Ephesians 4, and then only as one of a group of ministries within the church. If you look closely at New Testament church leadership, there is not a single example of a church being led by one man. In every case, whether it is Jerusalem, Antioch, or Ephesus, a plurality of leaders is described. In Acts 14, we see Paul and Barnabas returning to the churches they had planted and appointing elders (more than one) in every church. So we see that local church government was by a group of leaders.

What were the qualifications that these leaders were supposed to have? It was not a seminary training, or a degree in theology. In I Timothy 3 and Titus 1, there is a description of the necessary qualifications to be a leader. The focus is far more on issues of character and lifestyle than anything else. It was, and remains, far more important for the church to be led by men and women of character and integrity than charisma! How different today, when the ability to entertain (whether in preaching or leading worship) from the platform is the major ingredient in the choice of pastor or worship leader. The search committee may be able to offer the right salary to draw away a person from another church, but this hardly constitutes a call from God!

There is an incredible safety for those in leadership, when the church is run along New Testament lines, by a group of leaders. I remember when Tony was doing a huge amount of national and international travel tied up with the ministry that he ran among physicians and other health care professionals. He was also one of the leaders of the church we were a part of in the East End of London. The leadership team of our church in London decided that he was away far too much, and that our family life was suffering. (Now, I had been telling him that for months!) God was blessing incredibly wherever he traveled. Yet, because he was a part of a team that willingly submitted their lives to each other, he

73

agreed that he would only ever be away for a maximum of two Sundays in any given month. I praise God for the collective wisdom of that leadership team! If leaders were genuinely a part of an inter-submitted team which practiced a mutual accountability, I very much doubt if we would have seen half the church scandals that have so devastated the church in the States in recent years.

Let me describe to you a little of the way these leadership teams have worked. It has proven to be a successful model in establishing a variety of churches in different countries and cultures. We meet on a regular basis, giving the majority of the time to worshiping and seeking the Lord. The more business things we have to cover, the more important it is to spend extensive times in His presence. If we fail to do that, it invariably takes us hours just to cover a few details. If we spend an hour or more in His presence, we can cover a huge amount in a very short time, because we will all be of the same mind. Added to this, the Lord is free to break in, and frequently does so, giving us prophetic words or insights that may totally change the course of the leadership meetings. I well remember our early experiences of leadership meetings that followed this pattern. In those days, one would never dare go into a meeting with unconfessed sin, because the Holy Spirit would invariably break through in some way to reveal and deal with it. Scary but awesome! Church leadership is not only seen in the context of the local church. Clearly Paul and others, such as the council of Jerusalem (Acts 15), had authority that went far beyond the local church, both through their force of personality and through their apostolic office. It is clear that the Lord is again producing in His church, worldwide, a respect and expectation that similar giftings are still being released into the body of Christ. What people like Peter Wagner call "the new apostolic reformation" is really just recognition that throughout church history God has raised up apostolic and prophetic men and women to help with spearheading His work.

William Burton, pioneer Pentecostal missionary to the Congo (Zaire), left over a thousand churches established by the end of his life. John Wimber, founder of the Vineyard movement here in the United States, may have been hesitant to use the term "apostle" to describe his own ministry, but many others would recognize him as fitting that office. Watchman Nee, whose sermons on church life were put together in a little book called *The Normal Christian Church Life,* describes very clearly the role of apostles and prophets. Watchman Nee left behind an indigenous church movement that has touched millions in China. His work also laid the foundation for many of the new churches that have emerged around the world.

You do not have to think that modern day apostles are of the same category as the twelve apostles to believe that apostles are for today. Clearly, this generation needs every gift that the risen and ascended Christ wants to pour on His church.[50] The church is still built on the "foundation of the apostles and prophets."[51] One of the weaknesses that we see as so prevalent in the smaller independent churches (meeting in homes and storefronts across this nation) is that they do not want, nor do they accept, the moderating influence of apostolic and prophetic ministries that come from outside their own fellowship. This leads to significant weaknesses. Suspicious of anything from outside, they tend to become insular and at times arrogant, and sadly, some, like the Exclusive Brethren of old, end up feeling that they are the only true Christians around. It doesn't take a prophet to discern that they might be wrong!

When local churches welcome the input of those they recognize from outside as apostles and prophets, they are availing themselves of a safeguard that the Lord has provided. Churches that remain open to outside ministry are less likely to become insular and inward looking. These churches are not limited by the gifting and ability of their own people, but can receive strength from those gifted ministries that Jesus has put into His body, to help His body grow and mature into "the measure of the stature of the fullness of Christ."

The apostle Paul, in writing to one of the churches, comments that, "even if you had ten thousand others to teach you about Christ, you have only one spiritual father. For I became your father in Christ Jesus when I preached the Good News to you."[52] An apostle is not necessarily viewed as being in the office of "apostle" by all of the churches that he or she visits. Paul "fathered" the church at Corinth, and as such was naturally viewed by the Corinthians as an apostle. Does this mean that everyone who has planted a church is apostolic in nature? Not at all. This would be no truer than saying that everyone who has given a word in prophecy is prophetic by calling. What does need to be recognized is that some are called as apostles and others as prophets. This is Biblical, and was a gift of the ascended Jesus to His church (Ephesians 4).

But since the purpose of the ministries listed in Ephesians 4 is to "release the saints for the work of the ministry," let's see how all of God's people become involved.

CHAPTER EIGHT

EVERYONE IS IMPORTANT!

While we were medical students, we were part of a rather unusual experiment in the hospital Christian group that we were a part of. Because everyone spent so much time together as a natural part of hospital life, we decided that we were actually functioning more as a church within the university than as members of whatever church we happened to go to on Sunday. So we took the step of calling ourselves a church. At the time this was viewed as rather controversial and ultimately led to our being thrown out of the Inter Varsity Fellowship. However, it did give us the satisfaction of a certain notoriety! Don't forget, this was the sixties!

Right from the start, we decided that our only textbook for how to run church was going to be the Bible. We set ourselves to study and see what it had to say about the church and church life!

God's original intention, as shown early in the scriptural narrative, was to have a people who would represent Him here on earth. In Exodus 19:5-6 it says, "Now if you will obey Me and keep My covenant, you will be My own special treasure from among all the nations of the earth; for all the earth belongs to Me. And you will be to Me a kingdom of priests, My holy nation." God's plan was to speak to Moses in such a way that the children of Israel could both watch and hear Him speaking, even though they were not allowed on the mountain itself. But when the children of Israel saw the lightning and smoke coming from the mountain, they were scared, and asked Moses to tell them what God said, rather than have Him speak directly to them. A direct relationship with God was proving to be rather frightening.

Later, at the beginning of I Samuel, the Israelites go even further and ask for a king: "Give us a king like all the other nations have."[53] When Samuel goes to the Lord about this, he is told by the Lord, "It is Me they are rejecting, not you. They don't want Me to be their King any longer."[54] It is not that different in our churches. Generally speaking, people prefer to be led than to have to put in the time and effort that is required to actively participate themselves. Even when it comes to hearing from the Lord, many would prefer a "word" from a passing prophet than to make the effort to really wait on the Lord for themselves.

Throughout the Old Testament there are hints that God is going to change this situation and get back to His original purpose. In Jeremiah 31, God describes the new covenant He plans to make with His people. "I will put My laws in their minds, and I will write them on their hearts. I will be their God, and they will be My people...For everyone from the least to the greatest will know Me."[55] God longs to restore that place of communion, of personal relationship, that He had with men and women in the Garden of Eden. How can a God who is described as "love" ever bear to be kept at arms length when it comes to relationship with His people, His children?

The New Testament pictures of church reflect this. I Peter 2 talks about us being built by God into His spiritual temple. "What's more, you are God's holy priests, who offer spiritual sacrifices that please Him because of Jesus Christ."[56] Later, in verse 9, "You are a kingdom of priests, God's holy nation, His very own possession. This is so you can show others the goodness of God, for He called you out of the darkness into His wonderful light." It is clear that under the new covenant, we are to be the kingdom of priests that God originally told Moses would point others to God.

The most frequent picture that the New Testament gives of church is that of a body. This is not just any old body. This is the body of Christ. Romans 12 and I Corinthians 12 are the key passages here. The natural body has many different parts, each with their different functions. Yet each is necessary for the correct operation of the body. So it is with the body of Christ. All of us are like different parts of a spiritual body. Each of us has different functions, all of which are totally necessary for the body's correct functioning. None of us can manage without the others. If one member is not functioning properly, then the body is weaker because of it.

When Tony came to England in 1967, he went his first Sunday to Westminster Chapel, the famous church then pastored by Dr. Martyn Lloyd-Jones. After the meeting, one of the congregation of this huge church noticed that Tony must be a newcomer. They went up to him after the meeting and offered to take him out to lunch. Tony cannot remember one word of what Britain's most famous preacher had to say that day, but he has never forgotten the kindness of the family who asked him out for lunch.

Who is really the most important, the person who greets people coming into church or the pastor who gives the sermon? An ordinary family lived that day the words of Jesus, "When you did it to one of the least of these My brothers and sisters, you were doing it to Me!"[57]

Sadly, the church does not often work like this. In most churches it is all too easy for a newcomer to come in, week in and week out, and still not meet anyone at a personal level. We have allowed church to become a spectator sport when we were all meant to be team members out on the field playing the game! We sit in our pews, gazing at the back of someone's head, when we are supposed to be, as John Wimber put it, "doing the stuff!" Both I Corinthians 14 and Romans 12 list the sort of "stuff" that we should be doing—everything from prophesying and teaching, to working miracles! I Corinthians 14:26 gives the only description in the New Testament of how a meeting should be run: "When you come together, each one has..." All of us should come to meetings expecting to take part in what is going on.

Back in those early days while we were at medical school, we decided that the Holy Spirit was going to be the one to lead the meetings, and that each of us would bring our contributions and expect Him to somehow coordinate it all together. We sometimes had painful times together when it seemed that the Lord was not in attendance with us at all. I remember awful times of silence, not lost in His presence, but just hoping someone would do or say something! At times it was so bad we just went home. But, gradually, over the months, the presence of the Lord became more and more of a reality in the meetings. We learned the value of Spirit-led leadership of a meeting, and frequently we would experience the Holy Spirit orchestrating the whole time in the most extraordinary way. Soon we had visitors from all over the country coming to see what God was doing! Every week people were getting saved, filled with the Holy Spirit, and taking what they were experiencing back to other churches and Christian students groups around the country.

Since those days we have tried to maintain *sola scriptura* ("only scripture") as our guiding principle. The New Testament is the textbook for church life. It would often seem easier to run like other churches, to ask for a king (senior pastor) like all the other nations around us, but we have never seen this as a scriptural principle. There is no question in our minds that God's intention is for the church to have a structure that enables each person to develop to their full spiritual potential. Leadership, as has been discussed earlier in this book, was never designed to be by one person, but through teams of gifted people, releasing each member of the body to function in a beautiful way. One of the consequences of this is that we have always had an emphasis on small groups. Small is beautiful! In the small group there is the potential for every person to take active part in a meeting. There is no better way to learn how to follow the Holy Spirit than in the non-threatening atmosphere of a small group. Here a person learns to prophesy, to bring a teaching, to lead worship. It is a great training ground for ministry in every aspect.

Does this mean that there is no place for the large gathering? Absolutely not! Big is beautiful too. There is nothing more inspiring than a large celebration with hundreds, if not thousands, of people all worshiping the Lord together. We see in the early church the disciples not only met together from house to house, but also in the Temple. We know that the apostles taught not just in people's homes, but also in the larger context of the temple courtyard, the synagogue and hired hall.

Some may ask, with this emphasis on the small

group, what becomes of the kids? Too often the children are kept out of church meetings as being the "church of tomorrow," when actually they are the church of today. In our experience, the kids play a vital part, particularly in any times of worship, even if they subsequently go off to play or to their own more appropriate teaching time while the adults are discussing God's Word together. The kids will frequently start a song, or pray for those needing prayer, when they are allowed to participate. We have often seen their contribution bring the Spirit of the Lord directly into a meeting in such a way as to totally change the course of that meeting. The Holy Spirit is no respecter of persons—not by age or gender![58]

One of the consequences of expecting every person to be a functioning member of the body is that it releases people to start their own initiatives for the kingdom. For example, in our fellowship there are people who run evangelistic discussion groups at their places of work. One couple within the church runs web pages for people with marriage problems.[59] Another pair reaches out to prostitutes through a special ministry at Easter time.[60] Still others are touching housing projects, or organizing their own mission trips to Romania, or doing relief work in Mozambique, or volunteering work within local schools.

The purpose of the five-fold ministries described in Ephesians 4 is to equip (release) the saints for the work of ministry. People need to be encouraged, released and then supported in whatever ways the Lord directs them. It is amazing how much can go on, even through a relatively small church, when people are released to be a kingdom of priests unto God. Leadership primarily exists to empower and enable "every person ministry," not to showcase its own gifts. Leaders, by laying down their lives in practical service, enable the body to truly build itself up in love.

CHAPTER NINE

YOU IN YOUR SMALL CORNER AND I

IN MINE

Even a casual read through the New Testament gives the impression that the church back then was founded on loving, real relationships. In the last part of Acts 2, and again in Acts 4, there is a graphic description of the way in which the early Christians lived. They shared their meals together, shared their possessions, and shared their lives.

A very constructive exercise is to go through the New Testament looking for the "one another's." Amongst many other commands, we are told to lay down our lives for one another, to build one another up, to bear one another's burdens, to be kind and tender hearted toward each other, to admonish one another. These are not things that can be done while gazing at the back of someone's head in a Sunday meeting. They imply a vital sharing of our lives together, not just in meetings, but also day by day. Take the command to bear one another's burdens and so fulfill the law of Christ. [61, 62]

This means either that a person knows others in their church well enough to recognize when all is not well, or that a person feels safe enough to share the deepest things going on in their lives when they are hurting.

For several years after arriving in this country, we went to a variety of churches, some of them excellent in many respects. However, at two of those we attended (each for more than a year), apart from being greeted at the door, there was rarely any communication with any other person. Now some of that was our fault. We did not go out of our way to make friends for various reasons (mostly bad!), but no one went out of their way to try to draw us in. At one of them, I'm sure I was perceived as a single mom because Tony was working weekends. Since nobody ever saw him, they would have no reason to think I was married. I noticed a marked difference in the way that I was treated. This hit me especially hard because of what we had been used to in London in the church that we had helped to pioneer. There, things were arranged so that no stranger could leave one of our meetings without having received at least two invitations to someone's home for a meal. The culture is different, I know, but the principles are the same. At one point we nearly got involved in a church simply because in the week after we had visited, we received a couple of phone calls and a letter, and someone came round to bring some cookies and invite us to their home group.

The New Testament Christians obviously spent much of their time together. How can this be done in the busyness of American life today? Part of our problem is that we feel we can only invite others into our home if everything is perfect—not a speck of dust on the furniture, the kids all on their best behavior, and a cordon bleu, home-cooked meal sitting on the stove! If that is our standard, we will never get to know each other! Why not invite another family around for pizza before you take the kids to the ball game? Or invite a single parent and kids over just to share a movie? It will probably be the first invitation they have had for a while and might make your week!

When we lived in London, one of our home churches had several nurses in it, working really odd shift hours. We were in tough inner city London, and their only way home was to take public transport—not particularly pleasant late at night, to say nothing of the safety issues. That home church decided that they did not want those nurses using public transport late at night. So each week they would get the nurses' schedules, and someone would meet them with a car whenever they came off duty to make sure they traveled home safely. That's fine for the first week or two, but think of the commitment involved when this goes on month after month! Now that is a practical expression of laying down your life for someone else!

We personally experienced this kind of commitment when we had really young kids. One of the single girls in the church decided that her ministry to Jesus was to clean our house every week. That was no small task in a hundred-year-old, four-story, London terraced home where there were three young kids and an endless stream of visitors. She would not accept a cent in payment! It is very humbling when others lay down their lives for you in such practical ways. It also builds deep friendships.

It is hard to enjoy any sense of "community" when we see each other a couple of times a week for an hour or so, at the most. It is wonderful when Christians, desiring to share their lives in more meaningful ways, begin to so order their priorities that they can spend time together.

In the New Testament, the believers not only shared their time but also their possessions. None of them said that anything they had was their own, but they shared everything. Many years ago, we were challenged by A. W. Tozer's five vows, one of which was that we were never to own anything. This means that the Lord can do what He wants with my possessions. If He asks me to give something away, it is not mine to hold on to. The principle here is stewardship rather than ownership. I need to take good care of the things that are entrusted to me. I may need to think twice before lending out my possessions to people who I know will not return them in as good or better shape than they received them. But apart from that, my material goods are not my own. Think how many resources could be released into the kingdom if we shared, for example, our power tools, our lawn mowers, or our cars.

I (Felicity) will never forget another blessing that came our way. We were newly married and one of the people in the student church that we had helped to pioneer decided that we needed a car. Unbeknownst to us, she worked for the whole summer, and then presented us with her entire earnings. Imagine how surprised we were, how unworthy we felt, but also what an incredible blessing it was! And looking back on what that car enabled us to do as newly married students in a busy medical school context, I can see that we were able to touch many more people because of the travel time saved. She really had made her gift to Christ, and we were enabled by her generosity to live our lives more effectively for the kingdom.

Sharing ourselves is often the most difficult thing to do. Paul could say in I Thessalonians 2:8, "We loved you so much that we gave you not only God's Good News but our own lives, too." In our culture it is not acceptable to show weakness. We all go around wearing masks. We wear the mask of a bright smile and "everything's fine," when actually our marriage is falling apart. Or maybe we don't know how we are going to put food on the table this week, or we are scared that our kids are going out control, or we feel so depressed we don't know if we are going to make it through the day. The contrast to what has become the norm is illustrated by a passage such as I John 1:7 that tells us "if we are living in the light of God's presence, just as Christ is, then we have fellowship with each other, and the blood of Jesus, His Son, cleanses us from every sin." There is a transparency here, a willingness to let others see us as we truly are. Openness of this sort does make one liable to be hurt at times, but all loving relationships have the potential of causing hurt. Those we love the most have the greater capacity to hurt us. Does this mean that I won't accept love because I refuse to risk hurt? Jesus loved us so much that He laid down His life for us. Love covers a multitude of sins. It also builds us up into a living demonstration of the body of Christ.

Do we feel safe sharing our innermost selves with a trusted brother or sister? It can take a lot of courage. Or from the other side, are we able to respect confidences and to love unconditionally without judging? The book of I John is full of passages that talk about the need for us to love one another. Time and again it asks how you can love God, whom you cannot see, if you do not love your brother. Our love for God is to be measured by our love for our brothers and sisters.

Are we prepared to rise up to the challenge of meeting the New Testament standard of building our church on relationships rather than just attending meetings or being part of the program? Are we willing to be inconvenienced in our personal lives to do this? Are we prepared to take the children of the single mom for a day so that she can get some time off, or to take time to visit the person who is sick or in prison?

In John 13:35 it says that the world will know that we are His disciples when we love one another. Is it currently that surprising that not only the world, but even many Christians are dropping out of involvement with the church because they cannot find any real relationships there?

CHAPTER TEN

IT'S OK TO START A CHURCH

"Holly, we've missed you the last few meetings, is everything all right?" I (Tony) asked.

"I'd love to come with the kids, but Joe is currently working when you guys meet, and we only have the one car. Living so far away from the rest of you, we didn't want to inconvenience anyone by arranging a ride," was Holly's reply.

What do you do here? It is true that Joe and Holly live about fifteen miles out in the country, in a small community south of Austin. What should we do?

Well, how about starting a new church?

When I suggested this to Holly, her answer really surprised me. Joe had already told her that he was wondering if they should start a church in their neighborhood. She also mentioned that there were two other families who might come to a meeting in her home who immediately came to mind. Then, as she thought further, she remembered another family that she realized had stopped going to church over recent months that would probably come as well.

It has been shown repeatedly that one of the fastest ways for any church to grow is to plant new churches. Whether the church is large or small, the very act of planting a new church releases new life, and challenges the original church group to reach out to God for more. Because most people's concept of church planting has included buildings and full-time staff, the very thought of starting a new church is more than they can cope with. But move all of the expenses (not the sacrifice) out of the equation, and suddenly the impossible is quite possible.

David Garrison, in his excellent booklet, *Church Planting Movements,* published by the International Mission Board of the Southern Baptist Convention, describes many examples of very young Christians starting churches. [63]

The key seems to be the expectation that this is normal. Then add the wisdom and encouragement of those who have gone before to build it into the very DNA of all emerging churches. The New Testament is filled with examples of Paul visiting a locality for a very short time and then moving on rapidly to the next place. He trusted the Holy Spirit to lead the new converts effectively. He was not looking to set up his own empire, but entrusted them to God's kingdom. Clearly, the rapid expansion of the gospel message that was the norm in New Testament times, and which continues in many countries today, is linked to ordinary believers reaching out effectively. When we understand that "church" is starting when two or three families are meeting together in Jesus' name, then almost anyone being led by the Holy Spirit can help facilitate that!

Recently, Felicity and I were in India speaking at a series of conferences on starting churches. We had pastors and evangelists, teenage girls, and elderly men, people with PhD's and people who were illiterate all sharing in the seminars. Many of them had already been involved in church planting. Some had planted several churches. The distinguishing mark of those who had started churches was not their great learning but their great passion.

Shanti was a priestess to her fishing village community, serving the Goddess of Wealth. From an early age she had tried to serve her gods by spending hours in worship at the local shrines, where she was revered for her spirituality. One day her brother, a recent Christian convert, gave her a picture of the Holy Spirit descending as a dove on Jesus at His baptism. Shanti added this picture to her shrine of idols and began to worship the picture along with her other gods.

One day, while worshiping the picture, a bright light came and filled the room. For hours she was lost in the presence of the living God. At the end of this experience she knew something had happened. She shared this with her brother who explained to her that she had become a Christian through the saving work of Christ. She renounced her idols, and was promptly beaten up by the local Hindu priests. Her husband completed the work by throwing her out of the house. Now destitute and homeless, she lived by begging for six years, giving much time to prayer and fasting whenever there was no money for food.

At the end of this six-year period she felt that God was leading her to accept the challenge of feeding at least ten people a day, even though she was just a beggar herself. From this inauspicious start, right in the village where she had been thrown out of the local temple, she had, within a few years, built up a congregation of two hundred villagers who were followers of Jesus. Every week, a band of about fifty young people, who are a part of this emerging church, go out with her to the surrounding villages and share their testimony of what the Lord is doing in their lives.

In the two weeks following the church planting seminar in which she and a number of the young people were in attendance, they started a half a dozen new churches. Wow! What's our excuse? Felicity and I were so challenged by others' response to the things that we had been trying to teach that the Lord has used it to push us out into radical and rapid church planting activity. In the same two week period we have seen two new churches emerge, and have done the groundwork to help two or three other groups get up and underway in the immediate future.

God's people need to be released. Who says that you can't start a church? The Holy Spirit and His Word say that you can. In Acts 16:5 we read how the churches grew and multiplied daily. This may be reading things into the passage that some would say are not there, but can't it literally mean that churches were starting every day? You can't do that when your concept of church growth is dependent on a building program and finding full-time helpers, let alone training them.

In Acts 8 we see what happens when Christians are pushed out of the nest. The death of Stephen (Acts 7) unleashed a time of severe persecution on the church. The result is startling! Acts 8:4 tells us, "The believers who had fled Jerusalem went everywhere preaching the Good News about Jesus." In no time at all, new communities of Christians were flourishing all over Israel and that part of the Middle East. It was only to be a small step for some of these new believers to cross the cultural divide and start sharing the good news with Gentiles (Acts 11:20). Will it have to take persecution before we can experience the same explosive church growth? It has been a hallmark of the church throughout the ages that when persecution does come, the true believers thrive! They may not enjoy the persecution. Who would? But the body of Christ grows strong in times of crisis. Within our own generation the extraordinary growth of the church in countries like China, Cambodia and Mozambique, to name a few, is proof enough of this fact.

The reality is that when the church is out of man's control, forced out of the box by persecution or deliberately released by apostolic and prophetic people who understand the role of leadership, that the church grows fastest. It may not be tidy. There will be problems. But they are the problems of life and not of stagnation.

Johnny and Rita have been a recent case in point. They turned up at our monthly celebration a year ago for the first time, having in a most extraordinary way found out about the meeting in our home. The Lord had been challenging them that they should start something in their home, but they didn't know if anyone had ever done that before. Were they allowed to start a church in their home? The celebration was a great time and Johnny and Rita told us that they would definitely be coming again. They were away for a couple of weeks after that on some planned time off, so we arranged for them to come over for supper after they arrived back from vacation. Imagine our surprise (and delight) when around the meal they told us that they were starting a church in their home that coming Sunday.

But wait! They hadn't asked our permission. We hadn't really had any chance to make sure that they were properly cemented into the existing home fellowships. Maybe their theology was going to prove rather unorthodox. These and many other thoughts were in our minds. However, the Holy Spirit had told them to do something, and they were doing it. Why would it need our approval? At the next monthly celebration they turned up with around ten people and, lo and behold, another church has been successfully established.

So, where do you start? Surely it is within your own sphere of influence. We started with all of our kids' friends. Every Sunday morning we would invite the kids in our neighborhood over for a huge breakfast followed by Bible study. We presumed that if they were on the streets on a Sunday morning, their families were not churchgoers. They may have come for the food, but they stayed for the friendship and fellowship! With our business contacts we began an evangelistic Bible study in the book of Proverbs. I told them to come so that we could think through what the wisest man who ever lived had to say about wealth. Within the year the twelve people who came to that business Bible study had all become Christians or re-committed their lives to the Lord.

Everyone has a neighborhood, a place of work, a circle of influence. Jesus taught us to pray, "Thy kingdom come, Thy will be done on earth as it is in heaven." For that to be a reality we have to be available to become an answer to our own prayers.[64] We must expect to help establish the kingdom (rule) of

God in every place that the Lord places us. When Felicity and I lived in the East End of London, our primary sphere of influence was medical. We were working in family practice. Our culture largely sees God as irrelevant. People in need do not often think to go to the church. Instead, they will go to see their family doctor. A loose translation of Exodus 15:26 says, "For I am the Lord, your family doctor." Could you not as a family doctor begin to open up with your patients about the Lord who loves them and who will bring true healing into their lives as well as their bodies? During our first few years in family practice we saw literally hundreds of patients give their lives to the Lord. They became the nucleus of the church that we were planting, and that church is still going strong twenty-five years later.

The role of apostolic and prophetic people, those gifted by the risen Lord (Eph. 4:7-11) to help in this church planting process, is another vital ingredient. They represent the maturity and the Biblical foundations that are necessary to help these emerging new church plants. Again referring to the excellent booklet *Church Planting Movements*, it is the sensitive and yet mainly hidden work of the apostles and prophets, these church-planting visionaries, which releases others into this work. As a child learns by having a parent model, teach, and then trust them to perform new activities, so we can be released into church planting by others for whom this is their call and passion. As each of us says to the Lord, "Here am I, send me," so we will find that every neighborhood, office complex, social class and strata of society can and will be reached for Jesus.

How do you get started? Pray, and keep praying. Begin to prayer walk in the neighborhood streets where you believe the Lord wants a new church to start.[65] Pray in the school that you are attending, asking the Lord to establish His presence there. We don't need permission from the Supreme Court to pray.[66] Talk to people about what God is putting on your heart. Ask God to lead you to someone else who shares your vision. We are much stronger when we go out two by two. In Luke 10, when Jesus sent out the seventy, he told them to go ahead of Him to every town and place where He was about to go. Wow! We are allowed to go and prepare the way for Jesus to come. We should expect, like those disciples of old, that we will find a "person of peace" who will open their home, classroom, or office to us because they also want to find out more about God.[67]

When the Holy Spirit gives you the freedom, just start the new church! The Holy Spirit will lead you. Ask for help from others who have trod this path before you. Welcome input from those more experienced than you. Develop relationships with them. Expect the house churches that you start to be starting other house churches immediately. Build this into your DNA. Don't try to control, instead try to release. Plan to be aggressive in your evangelism. People will only hear about Jesus when you talk about Him: "Faith comes from listening to this message of good news—the Good News about Christ."[68] Friendship is vital. People don't like being preached at but want to know that you care about them before you start trying to change them! Ordinary people who open up their homes and their lives are finding that they can start churches in their homes. Be hospitable. It is one of the cardinal rules for any leaders in a church.[69] Don't be intimidated by your lack of so-called qualifications. A call from God is enough!

So what do I do when I invite people over to my home (office/school/hospital) for a meeting? Well, don't panic, for starters. Jesus taught us that we don't even need to worry about what we are going to say, because the Holy Spirit will teach us what we need to say.[70] This is a home church. How about making everyone feel at home? The best way we know to do this is to always start with food. Even the meetings we have in the office begin with pizza! People open up over food. They relax and begin to talk about themselves and their situations. Create an atmosphere that is natural and into it bring Jesus as the centerpiece of conversation. Everyone coming knows they are coming to a "meeting." No one is going to feel that you are not allowed to put the focus of this time where you choose. Explain as you eat how you want to spend the time. Make sure that discussion, prayer, and Bible study is totally interactive. Don't monopolize the speaking. Draw everyone in. 1 Cor. 14:26 tells us that when we come together, "each one has" something to share, to contribute. You will be amazed to find that when you give everyone room to respond to what the Holy Spirit is doing in a meeting, your times together will have fantastic variety as well as excitingly relevant content.

We like to teach those that we are helping to start churches to Keep It Simple, Stupid: the KISS principal. Don't think of yourself as the leader so much as the facilitator. The Holy Spirit is going to lead if we will give Him room. Learn to cultivate a close friendship with the Holy Spirit. Talk to Him. Welcome His quiet whisperings in your own heart. Cultivate such a walk with the Lord that you may truly say in your experience that, "My sheep hear My voice," as mentioned in John 10. Encourage everyone, including those who aren't yet Christians, that their contributions are wanted and vital. Don't always have the answers. In fact, we encourage an atmosphere where what everyone says is important and valid, but that the answers need to be found in God's Word. Learn to point people to relevant passages of scripture so that the Word of God can speak for itself. Otherwise, you will give everyone the impression that it is what you say that is the final arbitrator of what is correct or authentic.

When the church begins to grow, encourage others to think about starting another church in their home. It is perfectly clear that the larger a meeting gets, the less likely everyone is to take part. By the time there are more people than will fit in most living rooms, maybe twenty or so, it is time to see another church begin. If you are still thinking leaders (i.e. pastors) and facilities (i.e. church buildings), then you will always limit how fast new churches can start. You can't start churches daily in a context where you need trained, full-time leaders or special buildings. But, as the number of home churches in any given region begins to grow, the day will come when we will see new churches beginning week by week, and in time, day by day.

As the wonderful Priceline.com ads say, "This could be big, really big." We pray so!

If you have enjoyed reading Simply Church *and would like to learn more about simple church structures, please visit www.simplechurch.com, or call (512) 282-2322.*

APPENDIX 1

RESOURCES AND MATERIALS

All the following resources can be ordered through House2House ministries by calling (512) 282-2322, or through our website at www.house2house.tv/store

1. *Church Planting Movements*, by David Garrison. Published and distributed freely by the International Mission Board of the Southern Baptist Convention (USA). www.imb.org

2. *Houses That Change the World*, by Wolfgang Simson.

3. *House2House* magazine, distributed on a free-will donation basis.

4. The *Getting Started* manual, compiled by Felicity Dale. A great introduction to starting home churches.

SIMPLE BIBLE STUDY METHODS

Method I—Three Questions

A few verses are read, and then the group answers three questions:

1. What does it say?
2. What does it mean?
3. What difference does it make in my life?

You may wonder if there is any difference between questions one and two. But take the phrase from John 1 where it says, "In the beginning was the Word." There is a huge amount of meaning in there that could get missed if the second question were not included. We use this method in our churches that meet in retirement homes. It is very simple and easy.

Method II—Three Symbols

This is a modified Navigators' method. A couple of verses are read, and we look for things that correspond to three different symbols: a question mark, a candlestick or an arrow. The question mark symbolizes something a person does not understand. The candlestick is used to represent something that sheds light, either on another passage of scripture, or else on something that is going on in a person's life. Lastly, the arrow stands for something that pierces a person's heart—they know that they have heard from God and need to do something about it.

For example, a person might say, "I have a candlestick on this verse. This describes a situation that happened to me at work last week..."

Method III—Open Discussion
This method we learned from Robert Fitts; it is used in his Alpha-Omega Bible Colleges (ABC's). Simply read the chosen passage of scripture, each taking turns reading a few verses, depending on how many people are present. Invite people to interrupt the reading at any time to make a comment or ask a question.

If it seems that too much is being read, then the facilitator will stop the person reading and ask, "Does anyone have a comment?" It is unusual for more than a few verses to be read before a discussion develops.

Our churches that meet in the housing projects use this kind of study.

Remember...
The method used is not important. It is just a tool to accomplish the goal of a participatory Bible study. Here the Bible itself is the teacher, and everyone in the group is involved in both the teaching/learning process and the application of what is learned to daily life.

END NOTES

[1] Check out Larry Kreider's message, *The Emerging House Church Networks*, for an excellent treatment of this subject. Available on cassette or CD from Dove Christian Fellowship Intl (www.dcfi.org).

[2] For more on this, see "Where in the World is the Church?" an article by Tony Dale, published in issue 6 of House2House magazine. It can be viewed online at www.house2house.tv

[3] Daniel 12:4.

[4] *TIME* magazine article during summer of 2000.

[5] In Mozambique, Rolland and Heidi Baker have seen more than 3000 churches established over the past 5 years.

[6] Sources such as Operation World (www.operationworld.org) and Dawn Ministries (www.dawnministries.org) provide good documentation of church growth worldwide.

[7] Acts 17:6.

[8] Ecclesiastes 1:9.

[9] Matthew 23:24.

10 Matthew 19:19.

11 1 Samuel 16:7.

12 2 Timothy 3:5.

13 Romans 12:5.

14 1 Timothy 3:15.

15 1 Peter 1:12.

16 A. W. Tozer was for many years the editor of the *Alliance Witness*. He was a great prophet of God, with a sharp mind and sharper pen. Any time spent in his books will be well rewarded!

17 Matthew 6:33.

18 Dawson Trotman was the founder of The Navigators, and he is much respected across all evangelical circles for his emphasis on personal evangelism and discipleship.

19 Matthew 26:40.

20 2 Corinthians 3:6.

21 Common/local language.

22 See *The Open Church*, by Jim Rutz, and *The Pilgrim Church*, by E. Hamer Broadbent, for further thoughts and documentation of these ideas.

23 Hebrews 5:12.

[24] Watchman Nee, the founder of the Little Flock Movement in China, was arrested by the communists, and he ultimately died, while still in prison, twenty years later. His writings, actually they are mainly compilations of his sermons, have had profound impact on Christians around the world looking for a return to a more Biblical Christianity. His biography, *Against The Tide*, may still be available in some countries.

[25] Acts 1:3.

[26] This section was first published in the series *When Christians Disagree*, published by Intervarsity Press, UK.

[27] For an example of miracles in today's world, see the article by Jim Rutz in issue 5 of House2House magazine, called "The Miraculous—Then and Now." Can also be viewed online at www.house2house.tv.

[28] Romans 14:17.

[29] Luke 11:20.

[30] Hebrews 4:1-2.

[31] Matthew 11:12.

[32] It is worth noting that science is not the ultimate arbiter of truth, nor is it a detailed statistical analy-

sis, but rather what the Word of God says.

[33] Many people, such as Robert Fitts, are currently opening healing rooms all over the world and seeing fantastic results. For more information on these healing rooms, or on Robert Fitts' other ministries, see his website: www.robertfitts.com

[34] John 3:8.

[35] 2 Corinthians 4:16.

[36] 2 Corinthians 4:11.

[37] John 10:10.

[38] I Thessalonians 5:23.

[39] For example, just this month a local 12-year-old girl with kidney rejection following transplant, whom the doctors had given up on, experienced a miraculous turnaround immediately following prayer.

[40] For more on this, see *The Spontaneous Expansion of the Church—And the causes which hinder it*, by Roland Allen. First published in 1927, this is a most insightful book that will richly repay the time spent by anyone able to find and read it.

[41] I Corinthians 6:20.

[42] 1 Corinthians 14:26.

[43] Acts 13:22.

[44] Romans 12:1(NASB).

[45] 1 John 4:20.

[46] Philippians 2:14-15.

[47] Psalm 19:1.

[48] Psalm 16:8.

[49] Acts 13:1-3.

[50] Ephesians 4.

[51] Ephesians 2:20.

[52] I Corinthians 4:15.

[53] I Samuel 8:4-5.

[54] 1 Samuel 8:4-9.

[55] Jeremiah 31:33-34.

[56] I Peter 2:5.

[57] Matthew 25:40.

[58] Two books that give a very helpful new look at this area are *Ten Lies the Church Tells Women,* by J. Lee Grady, and *For Such A Time As This,* by Martin Scott.

[59] www.themarriagebed.com

[60] www. themagdaleneproject.org

[61] Galatians 6:2.

[62] An extensive (although not exhaustive) list of the "one another's" of the New Testament can be found in the *Getting Started* manual, which can be ordered by contacting House2House: www.house2house.tv or (512) 282-2322.

[63] *Church Planting Movements* is a free booklet that may be requested through the International Mission Board's website, www.imb.org

[64] For more on this, see "Where in the World is the Church?" an article by Tony Dale, published in issue 6 of House2House magazine. It can be viewed online at www.house2house.tv

[65] A good resource on the subject of prayer walking is *Prayer-Walking: Praying On Site with Insight* by Steve Hawthorne and Graham Kendrick (to order, visit IMB's resource center at www.imb.org).

[66] See response of Peter and John in Acts 4:19-20.

[67] For more about this, contact House2House about the Luke 10 courses: www.house2house.tv or (512) 282-2322.

[68] Romans 10:17.

[69] 1 Timothy 3:2 and Titus 1:8.

[70] Luke 12:11-12.

Free subscription to House2House magazine!

Sign up for a free subscription of House2House magazine—a magazine about house churches, edited by Tony Dale. While you're at it, sign up a friend! Just fill out the information below. You may sign up as many people as you like (use additional sheets of paper if necessary). Then mail your list to:

House2House, PO Box 465, Manchaca, TX 78652-9824

Name _____

Address _____

City _____

State/Province _____

Zip/Postal Code _____

Country _____

Phone (_____) _____

Email _____

Name _____

Address _____

City _____

State/Province _____

Zip/Postal Code _____

Country _____

Phone (_____) _____

Email _____

SA27-SC